A Play by John Townsend

Series Editors: Steve Barlow and Steve Skidmore

Heinemann

Heinemann Educational Publishers
Halley Court, Jordan Hill, Oxford OX2 8EJ
A division of Harcourt Education Limited

Heinemann is a registered trademark of
Harcourt Education Limited

OXFORD MELBOURNE AUCKLAND
JOHANNESBURG BLANTYRE GABORONE
IBADAN PORTSMOUTH NH (USA) CHICAGO

© John Townsend, 2003

First published 2003

07 06 05 04 03
10 9 8 7 6 5 4 3 2 1

British Library Cataloguing in Publication Data is available
from the British Library on request.

ISBN 0 435 21360 1

Copyright notice
All rights reserved. No part of this publication may be reproduced in any form or
by any means (including photocopying or storing it in any medium by electronic means and
whether or not transiently or incidentally to some other use of this publication) without
the written permission of the copyright owner, except in accordance with the provisions
of the Copyright, Designs and Patents Act 1988 or under the terms of a licence issued by
the Copyright Licensing Agency, 90 Tottenham Court Road, London W1T 4LP.
Applications for the copyright owner's written permission
should be addressed to the publisher.

Illustrations by Martin Cater
Cover design by Shireen Nathoo Design
Cover illustration by Roger Langridge
Designed and typeset by Artistix, Thame, Oxon
Printed and bound in Great Britain by Biddles Ltd

Original illustrations © Harcourt Education Limited, 2003

Tel: 01865 888058 www.heinemann.co.uk

Contents

Characters   4

Scene One: **Late Night Horror**   6
            Ed
            Sam
            Teri

Scene Two: **Nightmares Are Us**   15
            Ed
            Sam
            Cheri

Scene Three: **A Match Made in Heaven**   24
            Ed
            Sam
            Deri

Characters

Ed runs a scruffy old café in town. He is a bit rough and ready.

Sam has just left school but has no job. He is very boring.

Teri is loud, bossy, wildly dressed and very scary.

Cheri is tough, mean and ready for a fight!

Deri seems very nice – and normal! But she has a secret.

5

Scene One

Late Night Horror

Sam sits alone and fed up in Ed's Café – late at night. Ed goes to Sam's table to wipe it (with a dirty old cloth).

ED: We shut soon.

SAM: Right.

ED: You'd better be quick.

SAM: Right.

ED: I shut at ten on the dot.

SAM: Right.

ED: So what do you want?

SAM: A cup of tea. Make it two cups.

ED: Two?

SAM: In case she turns up.

ED: Who?

SAM: Teri. She said she'd be here.

ED: She'll have to hurry.

SAM: And some chips.

ED: All gone.

SAM: Hot dog. I'll have a hot dog.

ED: Too late.

SAM: Burger. I'll have a burger.

ED: They take too long.

SAM: Eggs on toast. I'll have eggs on toast.

ED: Eggs are off.

SAM: Beans on toast, then.

ED: You can have beans. No toast.

SAM: No toast?

ED: The bread is off.

SAM: Right. Just the beans then. With two teas.

ED: Cheer up, mate.

SAM: She won't arrive now. We never even met.

ED: You've never met her before?

SAM: Only on the Net. In a chat room: www.meet-a-friend.com.

ED: What does she look like?

SAM: No idea.

ED: So you made a blind date, eh?

SAM: We've sent messages. She says nice things.

ED: Risky. What does she say?

SAM: She likes fun, food and football. So do I.

ED: *Very* risky.

SAM: I don't think she's going to turn up now.

ED: My wife's free. You can take her out!

SAM: Teri could have been the one for me.

ED: Ssh. This could be her. High heels. I can hear high heels outside.

(They wait. Nothing. Ed goes to the kitchen.)

SAM: No such luck.

(The door bursts open. Teri falls in. She looks scary! She wears wild clothes, very bright hair, has nose studs and tattoos. She is LOUD!)

TERI: What a dump. Call this a wine bar? I'm Teri.

SAM: Er … Hi!

TERI: Get up off your behind and get me a drink. Get us a taxi to take us to a nightclub.

SAM: Er … really?

TERI: So you're Sam. You look a bit of a wimp. I'll soon sort you out. Give me a hug and a kiss.

SAM: But … er … I … er …

TERI: I won't eat you. Not yet! By the way … I told you lots of lies on the Net.

SAM: Oh.

TERI: That's the only way I can get to meet a boy.

SAM: I see.

TERI: I never eat cheap food. This blind date will cost you. Lots!

SAM: Never!

TERI: You want to see me when I've had six gins …

(Ed comes out of the kitchen with a tray.)

ED: Two teas and beans. We shut in two minutes.

TERI: Get lost, mate. No one tells me what to do.

ED: You what?

TERI: And that tea looks like it's from a sewer.

ED: Well, it looks as if you should know, love.

(There is a tense silence. No one moves.)

TERI: *(Shouting at Sam)* Well, do something, you fool. You can't let him say that to me …

SAM: Er … well …

TERI: Hit him. Thump him. TELL him. NOW!

SAM: Right. I'd like to say …

TERI: Show me that you love me.

SAM: I'd like to say … those beans look good.

TERI: WHAT?!

SAM: I like this café and Ed's food. It's cheap.

ED: Teri doesn't think so, lad.

SAM: *(Trying to act)* Teri? Who's Teri?

ED: You told me you were waiting for Teri.

SAM: No, not *her*. I've been waiting for *Terry*. Terry is my brother. I can't think where he is.

TERI: But you're my blind date.

SAM: You must have got the wrong person.

TERI: I've come here to meet Sam.

SAM: My name isn't Sam. I don't know who you are. I never want to see you again. *(He runs out)*

ED: He's left his beans.

TERI: I've been stood up!

ED: This cup of tea will cheer you up.

TERI: *(She sips from the cup and sulks)* All I got out of this is a cup of lousy cold tea!

ED: Not quite. You've got this as well.

TERI: What is it?

ED: Well, someone's got to pay. It's the bill!

(Blackout)

Scene Two

Nightmares Are Us

Ed's Café is empty. Ed is in a mess. He has buckets, mops and a sink plunger. Sam runs in, in a good mood.

SAM: Quick.

ED: Eh?

SAM: Hurry.

ED: You what?

SAM: I'm in a hurry.

ED: Oh yeah?

SAM: I haven't eaten all day. Ten minutes.

ED: Ten minutes?

SAM: She'll be here in ten minutes.

ED: Who?

SAM: The girl of my dreams.

ED: In ten minutes?

SAM: Food. I need to eat. Fast.

ED: Fast? I don't do fast.

SAM: I need to eat before she gets here.

ED: Why don't you wait for her?

SAM: It'll cost more. I'll have to pay for her as well.

ED: You know how to treat a girl!

SAM: I need food first. Or I'll feel wobbly.

ED: Wobbly?

SAM: I won't be at my best. Can I see the menu?

ED: It's on the wall.

SAM: There's not much on it.

ED: I'm busy.

SAM: There's a bit of a funny smell.

ED: That's why I'm busy. Trouble.

SAM: Trouble?

ED: Yeah, trouble. With the drains.

SAM: What sort of trouble?

ED: Blocked.

SAM: Blocked? You need a plumber.

ED: Really? I never thought of that.

SAM: Can you get me a cup of tea?

ED: It'll taste funny. The kitchen is under water.

SAM: Not to worry. I don't mind.

ED: I do. The fridge is full of sludge.

SAM: Five minutes.

ED: Five minutes?

SAM: She'll be here in five minutes. I'll have Today's Special with gravy.

ED: It might be lumpy.

SAM: I don't mind. So long as it's hot … and cheap.

ED: I'll see what I can do.

SAM: Have you got frogs' legs?

ED: No, I always walk like this.

SAM: No, real frogs' legs. They'd be just the job.

ED: Really?

SAM: I think she's French. She'd like frogs' legs.

ED: Today's Special is a bit like frogs' legs.

SAM: Her name's Cheri. Sounds dead sexy.

ED: So does Today's Special. It's 'toad in the hole'.

SAM: I've never really met Cheri. Only on the Net.

ED: Not another blind date.

SAM: This one's special. She's got class. And taste.

ED: Just like my toad in the hole … *(He goes into the kitchen)*

SAM: *(He combs his hair… and his eyebrows)* I bet she's so silky and sleek. I can't wait …

(The door bursts open. Cheri leaps in. She's in army combat uniform. She's got a big rucksack with pans tied on.)

CHERI: Are you Sam? *(She grabs him by the collar)* Yes or no?

SAM: Er … Yes.

CHERI: Then get me a pie – and step on it.

SAM: But that will squash it.

CHERI: *(She grabs him again)* Listen, mate. I don't do jokes. I'm hungry. I'm mean. I'm Cheri.

SAM: It's a pretty name …

CHERI: Listen, mate. I only said I'd meet you so I could rip you apart. I'm in the SAS and I have to kill ten men to get my badge.

SAM: Really?

CHERI: Yeah. I've already done nine.

SAM: Oh. You're not French, then?

CHERI: I want food. I've been hiking all week. I sleep rough in the woods. I kill to live.

SAM: Oh dear.

CHERI: Last night I roasted a toad on a stick.

SAM: You can't beat 'hole in the toad'!

CHERI: *(She grabs him again)* I've told you once. I don't like jokes.

SAM: *(Whispers)* And I don't think I like blind dates.

CHERI: I've got a tent in this sack. You're camping out with me tonight. I'll see if I like you.

(Ed enters with a plate covered with a cloth.)

ED: It's a nightmare in that kitchen.

SAM: It's no better in here. Is that my food?

ED: You can eat it if you like. Is this Cheri, then?

CHERI: What's it got to do with you?

ED: Would you like frogs' legs or toad in the hole?

CHERI: I only eat things that I kill myself.

ED: That's good. Help yourself. I found what was blocking the hole in the drain. Here it is.

(Ed takes off the cloth to show a big toad.)

ED: You can't beat a real TOAD IN THE HOLE!

(Sam faints. Blackout.)

Scene Three

A Match Made In Heaven

Sam sits alone and fed up in Ed's Café. It's early Saturday evening. Ed wipes Sam's table. It is cold.

ED: Have you got a match?

SAM: What?

ED: Have you seen a match?

SAM: Yeah. I've just been. They lost.

ED: Not a football match. A match.

SAM: Eh?

ED: For the boiler. It's gone out. I've got trouble.

SAM: So have I.

ED: Gas trouble.

SAM: I've got girl trouble.

ED: I need a good match.

SAM: I need a good girlfriend.

ED: Haven't you got one?

SAM: No. I'm meeting a new one here soon.

ED: No. I mean – haven't you got a match?

SAM: I've got a box of matches in my pocket.

ED: There's no hot water. Nor hot food.

SAM: I'd like a soup.

ED: There's only cold soup.

SAM: Or mash. Mash with gravy.

ED: There's only cold mash

SAM: Or mushy peas?

ED: Only cold mushy peas.

SAM: Yuk. Her name is Deri.

ED: Who?

SAM: The girl I'm meeting here.

ED: Is it another blind date?

SAM: Yeah. We met at www.meet-a-friend-dot-com.

ED: What's this one like?

SAM: No idea. She said she works in TV.

ED: That sounds good.

SAM: I don't believe a word of it. They all lie.

ED: She may be the girl for you.

SAM: I don't think so.

ED: It could be your lucky night!

SAM: Maybe it's my chance to be on 'Pop Idol'.

ED: More like 'Bone Idle'! *(He takes the matches and goes to the kitchen)*

SAM: It's just another dull night in at Ed's Café. What a waste of time.

(The door opens. Deri walks in. She smiles.)

DERI: Hello.

SAM: Hi.

DERI: It's a bit cold in here.

SAM: Yeah.

DERI: It's freezing.

SAM: The boiler's packed up. Ed will be out soon.

DERI: I'm looking for Sam.

SAM: Who?

DERI: Sam.

SAM: You can't be Deri. You look … normal.

DERI: Thanks. So you're Sam!

SAM: Yeah. I'd buy you tea but there's no hot water.

DERI: Not to worry. I've got another place in mind.

SAM: It's cheaper here.

DERI: Where I'm taking you is free.

SAM: I think I like you. That's odd …

DERI: What?

SAM: Out there. In the street. It's gone bright.

DERI: It's the lights.

SAM: What was that?

DERI: What was what?

SAM: I heard someone laugh.

DERI: Really?

SAM: Those lights are bright.

DERI: Shall we go where it's warmer?

SAM: Where?

DERI: To my work.

SAM: What for? Anyway, I bet you lied. You told me you work in TV.

DERI: I do. I'm working now.

SAM: You what?

DERI: Live. Those lights are TV lights. We're going out live.

SAM: What do you mean?

DERI: I saw your message on the Net and we came to get you for tonight's programme.

SAM: Eh?

(Ed comes from the kitchen – soot all over him.)

ED: It's no good. It's blown up. The match was useless!

DERI: We might find a perfect match later.

ED: Eh? Is this Deri? The girl of your dreams?

DERI: Not me. We have a line of young ladies waiting for Sam. You can come with us.

31

ED: Where to?

DERI: The studio. The show's going out right now.

ED: What show?

DERI: My job is to get the guests for the show. Our taxi is waiting. This could be Sam's big night.

ED: I wouldn't bet on it!

DERI: Sam, look into the camera. You're the next guest on tonight's show. Just step this way …

SAM: What show?

DERI: It's *BLIND DATE*, of course! We're on air. Come and meet the girl for you! Lights … Camera … Action …

(Applause. Cheers. Music. Blackout.)